KNIT YOUR OWN SKYSCRAPER
Tom Wombat

KNIT YOUR OWN SKYSCRAPER
was created and produced by The Watermark Press Pty. Ltd.
29A King St., Sydney, N.S.W. 2000

for

ANGUS & ROBERTSON PUBLISHERS
Unit 4, Eden Park, 31 Waterloo Road,
North Ryde, N.S.W. 2113
and 16 Golden Square, London WIR 4BN, United Kingdom

National Library of Australia
Cataloguing-in-Publication Data

Wombat, Tom.
    Knit your own skyscraper.

    ISBN 0 207 15238 1.

    1. Handicraft — Anecdotes, facetiae, satire, etc.
    I. Stomann, Allan. II. Title.

745.5'0207

Designed by Harry Williamson and Partners
Edited by Nom Deplume
Typeset by David Graphic Sales, Sydney
Printed by The Dominion Press - Hedges & Bell

KNIT YOUR OWN
SKYSCRAPER

by
TOM WOMBAT
Illustrated by
ALLAN STOMANN
and
KATRINA VAN GENDT

Angus & Robertson Publishers

For Thaddeus, Casey-Joe and little Chloë P.

CONTENTS

CROCHET YOUR OWN TENNIS RACQUET

Hi Hello! I hope you all enjoyed last week's little money-saving notion — the wedding dress woven from week-old potato peelings. I think you'll agree that given the heat on the 'SPECIAL DAY' our bride looked quite radiant, if a little uncomfortable. Pity about the odour.

Today I am going to turn my attention to a little saving that can be made on sporting equipment. Regular readers will remember the FUN we had with the home-baked cricket bats (didn't they put a little bit of icing on your life!) and the do-it-yourself footballs made from pigs' bladders (a bit messy, that one!).

Now its time for that most fashionable of sports — tennis. Its time to throw out those old-fashioned wooden racquets and bring in the new metal look! Yes! Look out McEnroe and Navratilova! When our Budget Bulletin readers get on the courts with their home-crocheted tennis racquets there'll be some stiff competition about!

YOU WILL NEED:
2 dead cats
1 No 4 crochet hook
2 wire coat hangers
6 fly papers

BEFORE YOU BEGIN:
Remove guts from cats. Stretch.

METHOD:
Bend coathangers into desired shape. Wind one cat's guts from side to side, then deftly thread the other cat's guts in and out, over and under and hey presto! One tennis racquet. Nearly finished now! Just wind the fly papers around the handle area for extra 'stick-tight' grip!
Next week we'll be looking at a DIY athletic support made from used tea bags. Make your man the talk of the locker room!

Bye for now!

Busy Bee

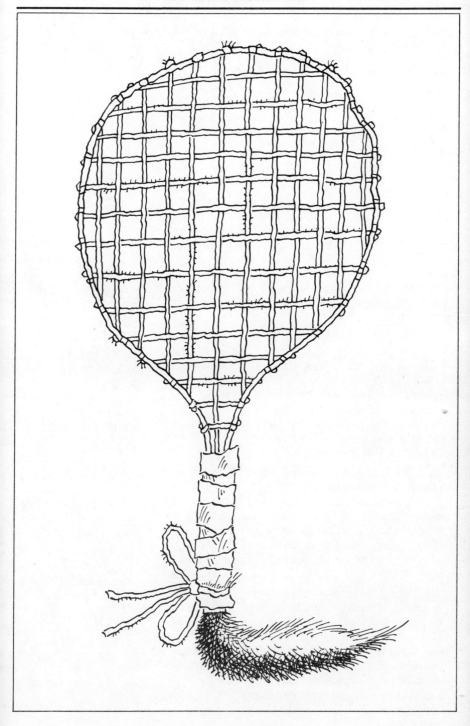

COLLECT YOUR

Well darlings, we all know how absolutely vital it is to be *in* – with the right set, doing the right thing, being seen in the right setting and so forth – and its this tricky area of the home environment where so many of you come unstuck. It is impossible to overemphasise the importance of hanging the right sort of paintings on your walls.

Take a tip from one who knows – you can't go wrong with the Impressionists – safe yet a little daring – so *right* for today's pastel decorator schemes – so much easier to blend in with the latest wallpapers than those lugubrious old masters depicting one's ancient relations that we all grew up with. Reproductions are absolutely out, of course, but the odd fake makes a good talking point as long as it is by someone colourful, like Emile de Hory.

First you need to find a good-looking art dealer you can trust with your cheque book. Secondly, if you want to be seen in the art world as a serious collector, you must select a theme. Some people mix and match their Impressionists with more modern artists – some even go as far as Jackson Pollock – but all those blotches and smudges are a little *unsettling* – not quite the thing!

I think it wise to stick to Monets – preferably those greeny-coloured ones with pinkish bits – so restful! so tasteful! so now! It can be such fun at the salerooms too; terribly exciting and one meets all one's friends – ooh another useful hint – do take along a hamper of goodies in case the bidding goes on through luncheon. Must fly!

OWN MONETS

Claude Monet

CARVE YOUR OWN SWIMMING TRUNKS

BE A REAL FASHION LEADER IN YOUR HAND-CARVED TOGS!

Get out your hammer and chisel and enjoy the built-in buoyancy that only the owner of a pair of wooden swimming trunks can enjoy. You'll be the envy of your friends . . . and you'll certainly stand out from the crowd.

EQUIPMENT:
(in order of appearance)
Adze
Calipers of a certain size
Mallet and croquet hoops
14-piece chisel set
1 tree
Grosses and grosses of rivets and roves
A certain amount of creosote
1 large spirit level, shaken — not stirred
A modest amount of hard core
A selection of rasps, clamps and ratchets

METHOD:
1 Measure distance from waist to bottom of bottom.
2 Measure circumference of waist and each individual thigh.
3 Take a slice out of an appropriately-sized tree, paying close attention to colourings, wood grain, knots, bark formations, rising sap etc. from both an aesthetic and comfort point of view.

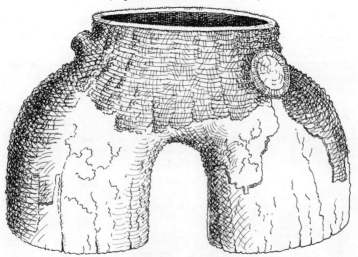

4 Chisel out your body shape from centre of log, paying particular attention to a snug fit in the crotch area.
5 Trim, plane, and sand the outside, and varnish with three coats of polyurethane.
6 Veneer the inside with a softwood such as balsa or baltic pine.
7 Stamp on logo with branding iron.
8 Why has no one thought of this before?

START YOUR OWN
RELIGION

The rewards can be considerable if you
go about it the right way — but before
you start here is a word of caution from
One Who Succeeded . . .

1 Verily, I say unto thee — thou
canst do it if thou really wantest.

2 But thou shouldst consider if
thou art prepared to go the whole
hog.

3 Because thou needest a large
back-up team and nigh on a
thousand years if thou wishest it to
catch on significantly.

4 And thine problems do not end
with thine own life.

5 In the hereafter, thou wilt be
forever pestered by Cecil B de Mille.

6 And thy flock are forever
wanting thee to do things for them
or being beastly to one another in
thy name which upsetteth one
mightily (but not as much as the
films of Cecil B. de Mille).

7 And another thing, huge
amounts of money will be spent on
thy behalf on gilded and twiddly
art treasures in dubious taste (I've
always been into performance art
myself) when thou wouldst rather
use the collection plate money to
sue MGM for misrepresentation.

8 Then one sitteth back and
relaxeth with a glass of altar wine
and what dost one hear? I'll tell
thee what one bloody well hears . . .
the casting department of MGM
arguing about what thou lookedest
like and what thou worest.

9 My basic gripe about all this is
that everyone thinkest I looketh
like Tab Hunter, weareth shapeless
linen shifts and haveth absolutely
no sense of humour.

Signed:
Disillusioned, Nazareth.

PSYCHOANALYSE YOUR OWN SOFA

1 Frame diploma and hang on wall.

2 Set timer for one hour.

3 Type up invoice.

4 Ask your sofa in, settle it down comfortably on soft surface.

5 Listen to what your sofa has to say.

6 Nod gently and mutter Aha! Um hum! at appropriate intervals.

7 Rise briskly when time is up and usher your sofa out of your consulting room. Do this, even if your sofa is in mid-sentence — this will help your sofa to become aware of the value of your time.

8 Type out more invoices. This will help you pay for all those little tax-deductable extras essential to the practising analyst, such as visits to Swiss clinics during the ski-ing season where you are bound to encounter all manner of rich sofas with suicidal tendencies and manically depressed, extremely wealthy chaise-longues.

PROFESSIONAL ETHICS: The importance of these cannot be overstated. You are bound at one point to become the love object of your sofa. Resist the temptation to lie on top of it even momentarily and do not perch on its seat or stroke its arms, as your sofa could misinterpret your motives and become so bitter and twisted that you may find yourself severely compromised.

When typing up invoices, use the tabulator to line up the columns of figures, this makes it much easier to add up the noughts and put the commas in the right places. It doesn't do to send out messy bills.

KNIT YOUR OWN SKYSCRAPER

Two delightful designs from one easy-to-follow pattern! Beginners will love the chunky lines of our basic 'Bauhaus-type' worker's block, which looks simply perfect placed beside a railway track on the approaches to an industrial town with a huge unemployment problem!

Imagine the fun of creating your own eyesore — your own patch of urban blight! Our version comes complete with vandalised lobby and lifts.

The more experienced knitter may like to try our 'Chrysler-type' building — an art deco masterpiece with some challenging cable stitch and double chain edges!

This elegant block looks good in high-rent business areas in major capital cities, and our pattern includes a preservation order *and* a controversial demolition order with more than a hint of organised crime involvement. This one will really test your twisting loops!

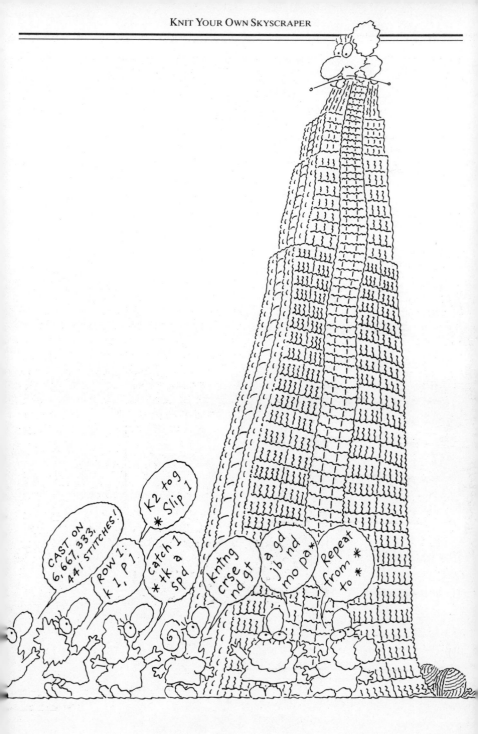

TENSION:

We believe this is inevitable if you are to tackle this project with any degree of seriousness, but if it gets too much, try unwinding with a stiff drink in a hot bath.

EQUIPMENT:

4 No 12 double-pointed knitting needles

A stitch counter

A theodolite

A crochet hook and bodkin

A house-full of relatives to maintain tension

500,000,000,000 balls of double-knit oiled wool

METHOD:

Cast on 6,667,333,441 stitches.

Row 1: K1,P1,K2tog* Slip 1, Catch 1* tk a spd knttng crse nd gt a gd jb nd mo pa* Repeat from * to *.
Continue until work measures 52 storeys.

Bauhaus beginners — it's time to cast off all consideration of human comfort and finish with a simple utilitarian water tower (see p94).

For those game enough to continue:

K1,P1* Slp wl rnd nd rnd nd rnd nd rnd nd rnd* Go fr lng wlk, casting off as you go. Repeat from** to **, creating hub-cap design of your choice, until work measures 77 storeys and only one stitch remains.

Slip 100 metre radio mast through last stitch. If knitting at home, transport to site and erect; if knitting on site, secure and prepare for topping out ceremony.

ASSEMBLING FINISHED GARMENT:

A crane may come in handy.

RE-ARRANGE YOUR OWN GENES

Tired of the way you look?
Fed up with the person you are?
In other words, are you sick to death of yourself?

Time was when in order to put things right you'd have to use all kinds of willpower — go on diets, take Charles Atlas body-building courses, enrol for Yoga, home-baking and macramé at night school and take assertiveness classes.

Lots of miserably unhappy people still flock to plastic surgeons, thinking that a nip and tuck in the flabby regions will alter their personalities and increase their brain power. We all know that's a load of rubbish. A nose job won't make you the Person Most Lusted After At Parties, but a genes job will.

A good genes job can alter every little inherited factor that bugs you from flat feet to pre-menstrual tension, from an ugly face to an ugly disposition, from a butterfly mind to a tendency to moodiness — and all thanks to Do-It-Yourself genetic engineering. All you have to do nowadays is fiddle about in the kitchen for an hour or two and re-build yourself according to your own specifications.

How is it possible?
Did you know that each cell in the human body carries all the information required to make up a WHOLE NEW PERSON!! This is the key!!

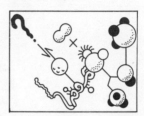

EQUIPMENT:

1 living cell from your body (do be careful!)
1 pair eyebrow tweezers
1 magnifying glass
1 test tube

METHOD:

1 Using your magnifying glass, identify nucleus of your cell. Here you should find 23 pairs of genes.

2 Now re-arrange them by poking them with the tweezers . . . you might try twitching at a seam here, doing up a zip there . . . it's all trial and error at this stage.

3 Pop your re-arranged cell into a test tube and top up with fertilizer. Keep in a warm place.

4 In a day or two, a new you will emerge from the airing cupboard. If you do not like the result, go back to step one.

N.B.
For disposal of unsatisfactory clones and/or original, see p94.

BEFORE: Yawn, yawn. Unassertive, overlooked and unmemorable.

AFTER: A dramatic transformation! A go-getting psychopath with unusual protruberances, terminal warts and hairy fingernails.

TAKE OVER YOUR OWN COUNTRY

Definitely a challenge, this one, but those who have completed this project do say success is sweet, if sometimes a trifle short-lived.

STEP ONE: FIND A COUNTRY RIPE FOR TAKEOVER

Worth including on any short list are countries whose cash crops include bananas, coconuts and rubber bands.

STEP TWO: DECIDING WHICH WAY TO GO

Establish whether yours is a left- or right-handed country. The smart will go with the flow — the brave may choose otherwise. (N.B. It is never too difficult to unearth pockets of discontent in hilly areas and slums.)

STEP THREE: GETTING EQUIPPED

FOR THE LEFT-HANDED:	FOR THE RIGHT-HANDED:
A beard.	A permanent 5 o'clock shadow.
Army fatigues (stained) and a can of 'instant sweat' spray for underarms and small of back. A large quantity of ammunition belts (*band-er-ill-oz* is what we call them from now on) to sling across the chest. Live ammunition optional. Judgement is required here.	A pair of jackboots, a set of gold epaulettes, a pair of white gloves, some kind of uniform and a great deal of medals. Much of this may be 'borrowed' from the doorman at your friendly neighbourhood Hilton.
Sunglasses with metal frames.	Sunglasses with metal frames.
Passing knowledge of Marx. For those short of learning time, the ability to recite one paragraph will enable you to get by. (This is called 'Going back to fundamentals').	A year's crop of bananas/sugar/copra. (This is called 'Economics').
A motley crew of supporters bearing mattocks and/or machetes. Looks are vital—your role models should be Sophia Loren and the young Fernando Lamas.	A wide circle of ageing Aryan friends to whom the mere mention of the word 'Nuremberg' causes perspiration to pop on brow.
Unending supply of half-smoked cigars with wet ends.	A lot of gold dental work, readily visible when smiling, grimacing or bursting into song.

Above: *Left or right?*
Below: *Right or left?*

Right: *Above or below?*
Left: *Right, left, right*

The ability to pronounce 'Guerrilla' like they do in Mehico and on the BBC.

A pleasing baritone.

Design new national flag, using primary colours.

Commission Andrew Lloyd Webber to write patriotic song (see above).

STEP 4: THE TAKEOVER

March purposefully into national radio or TV station. Ask to see the producer News/Current affairs. Address nation (in language of country if possible), choosing themes from either List A or List B according to persuasion or expediency.

LIST A:	LIST B:
Offer hand of friendship to China.	Offer hand of friendship to China.
Talk of equality, the people's rights, freedom of speech and the price of bananas.	Talk of grave economic crises, putting the country on the world map, purging the country of enemies and the price of bananas.
Abolish taxation.	Abolish taxation.
Denounce Margaret Thatcher.	Denounce Margaret Thatcher.
Pledge to hold cinema admission charges and announce tax concessions for film backers.	Announce increase in cinema admission and rescind import quota on Hollywood starlets.
Promise education reform.	Announce tax relief on school fees.
Invite Red Army Chorus to Cultural Festival.	Announce plans for staging 'The Ring'.
Invite Warsaw Pact and Third World Nations to Friendship Games.	Invite South African Rugby team to tour.

STEP 5: CONSOLIDATION

Now you are at the peak of your popularity, you must act fast. Both left- and right-handers will find themselves following the same set of instructions from now on (this is called 'Politics'). You must now nominate your ministers. It is wise to keep all the important posts to yourself — Prime Minister, Finance Minister, Home Affairs and so on. If you feel you can trust your husband/wife, make him/her the Minister of Culture. Make friends with and/or severely compromise your local CIA and KGB agents. Purchase tickets to Miami and/or Cuba. Pack your bags and keep them in the hallway. Open bank account in Cayman Islands.

STEP 6: RULE

Good luck.

RE-LOCATE YOUR

"Faint heart never re-located an airport"
ISAMBARD KINGDOM BRUNEL

STEP ONE: Locate centre of airport by measuring perimeter and drawing intersecting lines from meeting points of perimeter fences. Mark area of airport into one-metre squares by use of chalked strings, taking care to set at correct tension to ensure accurate twang (see p94). Calculate total number of square metres and hire this number of sturdy persons of uniform height – 5ft 9ins (162cm) is ideal.

STEP TWO: Tunnel under airport area working from one end to other in tidy line, taking care to leave uniform underpinning beneath airport sufficient to support runways, terminals and other heavy traffic areas.

STEP THREE: Position hired person with raised arms at centre of

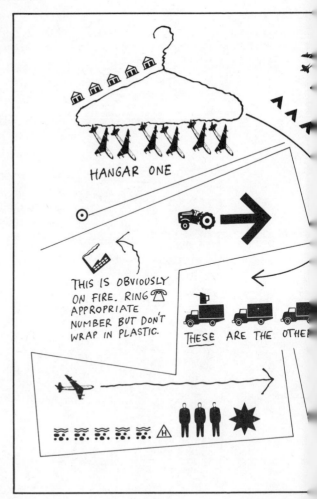

HANGAR ONE

THIS IS OBVIOUSLY ON FIRE. RING ☎ APPROPRIATE NUMBER BUT DON'T WRAP IN PLASTIC.

THESE ARE THE OTHE

OWN AIRPORT

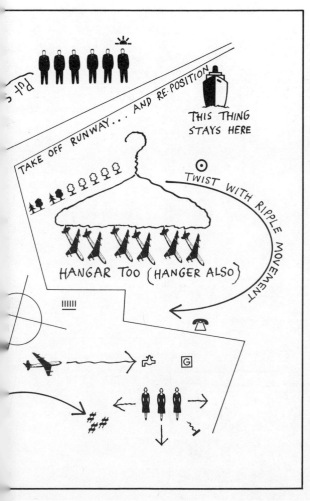

TAKE OFF RUNWAY ... AND RE-POSITION

THIS THING STAYS HERE

TWIST WITH RIPPLE MOVEMENT

HANGAR TOO (HANGER ALSO)

each square metre as you progress. Upon completion of tunnelling, disconnect services and instruct hired persons to proceed in direction of new location. It is advisable to pause during take-offs and landings. If transporting across water, ensure hired persons can swim.

STEP FOUR: Upon reaching new site, check alignment of runways in relation to prevailing wind and surrounding natural hazards. Shuffle airport into position by rotating around central point.

STEP FIVE: Place in new location with simple ripple movement to prone position, working from leading edge. Connect services. Darn wind sock. Collect IATA charges. (For release of hired persons from beneath airport, see p94.)

27

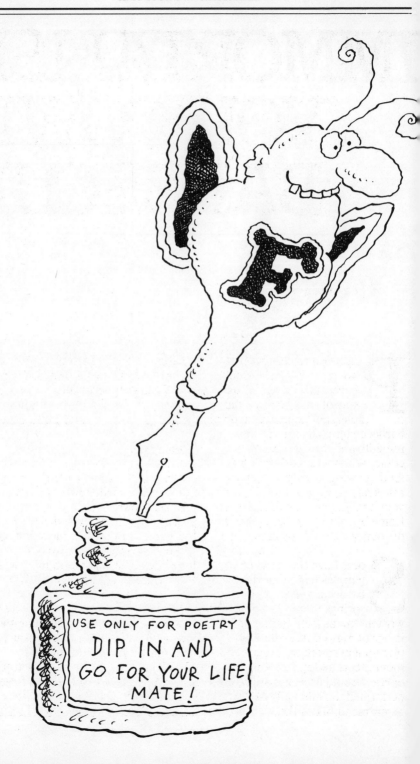

28

IMMORTALISE YOUR OWN BARBECUE

Publishing a slim volume of poetry in praise of your barbecue is a nice, tasteful way of ensuring that the pleasant hours you and your barbecue have shared will be remembered for generations to come. When your barbecue is just a fond, glowing memory and your ashes have grown cold in their urn, your descendents can re-kindle the flame by raking through the embers of your poetic endeavours.

Some have chosen to erect temples to honour their barbecues (The Taj M'Barbie springs to mind). Some have written operas (The Barbie of Seville is one of many). But complex planning permission is required for monuments and, unaccountably, operas about barbecues are rarely performed. So all in all, we recommend that if the coals of your barbecue are to burn on into posterity, the poetic route is the most likely to produce results.

Equipment:
1 pen
1 pad of A4 paper (ruled)
1 bunch daffodils
9 bean rows
An opium habit (optional)
1 publisher (you can pick them up quite cheaply at L'Escargot in London, the Algonquin in New York or Kinselas in Sydney)

Method:
A good beginning is essential, then all you have to do is keep going to the end, bearing in mind the rudiments of rhyme and rhythm . . . here are a few opening lines to get you going:

I wandered lonely as a sausage
That floats on high o'er grill and hearth
And all at once I saw a crowd,
A host of Foster's lager tins . . .

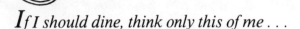

If I should dine, think only this of me . . .

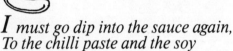

I must go dip into the sauce again,
To the chilli paste and the soy
And all I need is a large pork chop
And a napkin to hold it by.

Are there any more steaks said the traveller,
Knocking at the old inn door . . .

Is this a kebab I see before me?

To grill or not to grill, that is the question
Whether 'tis tastier in the end to fry
The chops and sausages in the same pan
Or to separate them from one another
And by grilling, cook them? To fry- to grill-
No more; but by a marinade to say we end
The toughness and the thousand chewy mouthfuls that
Flesh is heir to.

Theirs is not to reason why
Theirs is but to grill and fry.

COOK YOUR OWN CARPET

An extract from
'French Carpet Cookery'
by Bette Davide

One of the finest carpets or *Tapis* I ever enjoyed, was in the house of some dear friends near Aubusson. It was created one Christmas Eve in the chateau kitchens by the neighbourhood peasantry who had, of course, been cooking their own floor coverings for years. The aroma of that carpet will haunt me forever — a hint of tarragon in the alcove, a suggestion of garlic around the fireplace and the heady sweetness of oregano in the doorway.

I have adapted this traditional recipe for modern times, taking into account the lack of servants and restricted kitchen space. A word about the mozzarella. The original recipe calls for buffalo-milk cheese that has been curdled under a yak's armpit for at least a year. However, I have found Safeways Own Brand an adequate substitute.

This recipe will yield sufficient tasteful natural Berber for an average three-bedroom semi. Those with a taste for patterned Axminsters, sculptured weaves or shagpiles may find a recipe to suit them in the pages of the cheaper womens' weeklies.

Take two tonnes macaroni, penne or rigatoni, 50 kilos of mozzarella cheese, a dozen truffles — thinly sliced (at a pinch, finely chopped black olives would do), a fistful of oregano and 2 armfuls of haricot beans, soaked overnight. The best cooking pot is, of course, the traditional *tapisière,* but any 250 gallon earthenware crock with dimpled sides, convex bottom and a close-fitting lid will do. Put all the ingredients into your *tapisière* stir slowly with a *cuillère de bois* (wooden spoon), seal the lid with a flour and water paste and allow to simmer in a moderate oven overnight.

The following morning, assemble family and friends to witness the *dégorgement*. Tap the side of the *tapisière* sharply with a *marteau* (hammer) cracking the pot cleanly so that your carpet flows out onto the floor — step clear and when the mixture has cooled, smooth over with a spatula, pushing the mixture well into the corners. Trim edges with a pastry cutter.

Serve with finely-cut slices of *meubles* (three-piece suites) and a sprinkling of *tables occasionelles* (coffee tables).

HOW TO HUNT A GOLF COURSE

Real men club golf tees to death single-handed
Macho Hemmingay

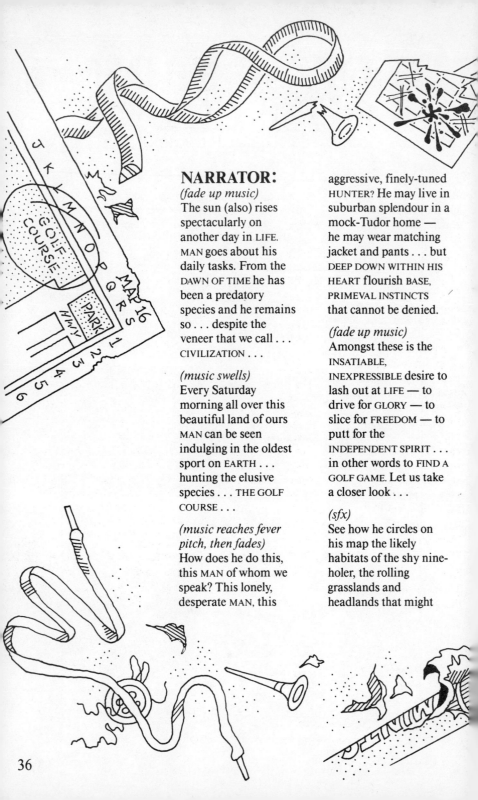

NARRATOR:

(fade up music)
The sun (also) rises spectacularly on another day in LIFE. MAN goes about his daily tasks. From the DAWN OF TIME he has been a predatory species and he remains so . . . despite the veneer that we call . . . CIVILIZATION . . .

(music swells)
Every Saturday morning all over this beautiful land of ours MAN can be seen indulging in the oldest sport on EARTH . . . hunting the elusive species . . . THE GOLF COURSE . . .

(music reaches fever pitch, then fades)
How does he do this, this MAN of whom we speak? This lonely, desperate MAN, this aggressive, finely-tuned HUNTER? He may live in suburban splendour in a mock-Tudor home — he may wear matching jacket and pants . . . but DEEP DOWN WITHIN HIS HEART flourish BASE, PRIMEVAL INSTINCTS that cannot be denied.

(fade up music)
Amongst these is the INSATIABLE, INEXPRESSIBLE desire to lash out at LIFE — to drive for GLORY — to slice for FREEDOM — to putt for the INDEPENDENT SPIRIT . . . in other words to FIND A GOLF GAME. Let us take a closer look . . .

(sfx)
See how he circles on his map the likely habitats of the shy nine-holer, the rolling grasslands and headlands that might

36

conceal a nineteenth hole, the recreation grounds in which a dangerous crazy golf game may lurk unseen . . .

(sfx)
See how our intrepid hunter, unafraid of the danger ahead, takes his lever-action number five iron and his centrefire bolt-action putter from the rack, dons his hat of Lincoln green and his uncomfortable new plus-fours. In the dawn's early light *(fade up music)* he sets off . . . stealthily tracking his prey . . . approaching from downwind like the true hunter he is . . . inspecting footprints and droppings.

(sfx)
The wise hunter knows that he must keep his ears open as well as his eyes . . . he listens for the tell-tale sounds of mowing machinery, the deep-throated curses of the less able players, the thwack of wood on plastic, the gurgle and hiss of gin meeting tonic . . . and finally he is rewarded . . . emerging from the rough he sees *(fade up music)* fluttering beguilingly in the breeze . . . his quarry . . . a small triangular flag.

(music swells)
Seizing his wood and his putter, he leaps onto the green sward, *(music climaxes)* hurls the flag to the ground . . . *(fade music)* It is over. He stands triumphant. THIS IS THE MOMENT TO SAVOUR. THE NEXT SLICE IS HIS . . . AND HIS ALONE.

HEW YOUR OWN GRANITE

TOP HOMES MONTHLY

You may remember the interview we ran a few issues back with Top Persons' architect, Mies van der Slabb. Well, we are reprinting edited highlights by popular demand:

THM: Good morning!

MvdS: Well, that all depends on the height of the slits in the walls *vis à vis* the angle of the sun . . . and would you mind leaving your pens and pencils and pieces of paper in your car . . . they clutter the place up.

THM: Er . . . yes . . . right . . . your first famous buildings were er . . . high-rise apartments that have since been condemned as unlivable-in and um . . . I think they've been pulled down, haven't they?

MvdS: I've never let buildings get on top of me. I'm into meaningful statements and what was meaningful for the masses then, I agree may not necessarily be meaningful now, but that in no way invalidates the pure conceptual essence of the original brutalist statement. Times were much more brutal then . . . there weren't as many private commissions for one thing.

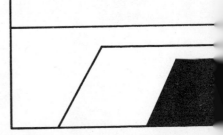

THM: Ah . . . yes . . . um . . . what I think our readers would be interested to know . . . is a little something about your present home. Here we are sitting in your . . . charming underground granite bunker . . . very innovative . . . very um.. interesting.. I'm

DINING TABLE

wondering . . . any decor tips on dealing with this . . . kind of um . . . you could say extremely sparse home?

MvdS: Environment . . . please don't use the word home. Well, of course, times are much more brutal and serious now, and my environment reflects this. Basically I've rejected other people's art in favour of my own. Who needs books and paintings and other such clutter when you can enjoy living inside a functional granite sculpture like mine? The dining table and seating environment over there may look like just another set of slabs to you . . . but there is an ergonomic element to the design. My clients appreciate this attention to detail.

THM: You must entertain a lot . . . maybe we could photograph you and your friends at dinner?

MvdS: Never, we never eat here — it would clutter the place up. We eat out.

THM: Ah.. maybe we could see the kitchen . . . bathrooms . . . bedrooms . . .

MvdS: We don't use such bourgeois definitions here. Basically all human functions take place within these interlinking, free-flowing spaces. In fact many is the night I've curled up on the dining table slab mistaking it for the sleeping slab, and you could say the shower cubicle does look rather like the garbage chute, but this is deliberate . . . a deliberate blurring of functions is what I am after.

THM: What about your clients . . . how do they feel about sleeping on the wrong slab?

MvdS: We've not had any complaints . . . but then not many people are sufficiently committed to actually live in my homes . . .

THM: Um . . . what does your family think about this . . . er . . . environment?

MvdS: Family? We never had children . . . they clutter the place up.

THM: Your wife?

MvdS: Er . . . my wife . . . er . . . yes . . . well, she lives in a hotel around the corner.

We were inundated with letters after that interview. It seems that millions of 'Top People' want to create, in their own homes, the subtle ambience that caused the little lady to pack her bags. I am told by Mies, that it was the granite dining table that proved to be the proverbial straw that broke the back. Here's how it's done:

1 Locate granite quarry.
2 Reinforce your floor before you effect delivery of huge slab to home.
3 Position slab in its final resting place as you will never be able to move it again.
4 Decide once and for all how many diners you wish to accommodate, as granite tables provide little flexibility on this score.
5 Sculpt on site, using a lot of noisy, messy equipment without dustsheets or suppressors.
6 Design table top with an interesting camber effect so that any clutter (i.e. knives, forks, plates of food etc) falls right off.

SEW YOUR OWN SHERMAN TANK

Cutting pattern:

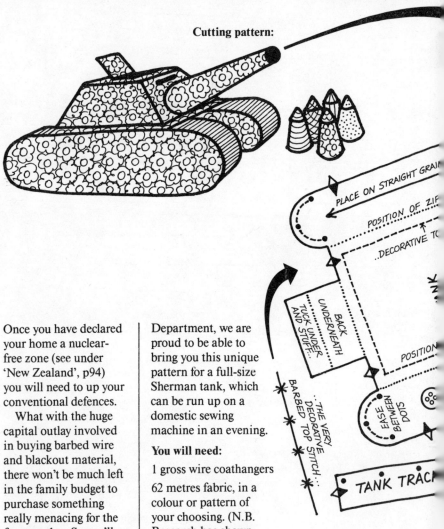

PLACE ON STRAIGHT GRAIN

POSITION OF ZIP

...DECORATIVE TO

BACK UNDERNEATH TUCK UNDER AND STUFF...

POSITION

...THE VERY DECORATIVE TOP STITCH... BARBED TOP STITCH

EASE BETWEEN DOTS

TANK TRACK

Once you have declared your home a nuclear-free zone (see under 'New Zealand', p94) you will need to up your conventional defences.

What with the huge capital outlay involved in buying barbed wire and blackout material, there won't be much left in the family budget to purchase something really menacing for the front garden. So you'll have to improvise.

In conjunction with the Defence

Department, we are proud to be able to bring you this unique pattern for a full-size Sherman tank, which can be run up on a domestic sewing machine in an evening.

You will need:

1 gross wire coathangers

62 metres fabric, in a colour or pattern of your choosing. (N.B. Research has shown that the general air of menace is somewhat dissipated if the tank is

made up in a floral print or a fabric intended for nursery curtaining.)
6 buttons
An assortment of cotton reels
2 extremely long zips

Method:
Stitch the front bits to the back bits in the usual way. Turn the finished tank inside out. Stiffen the structure with a framework of coathangers and slip the zips around the bits where you would expect the tracks to be. Button up the hatch and fill with air using the outlet of an ordinary vacuum cleaner.

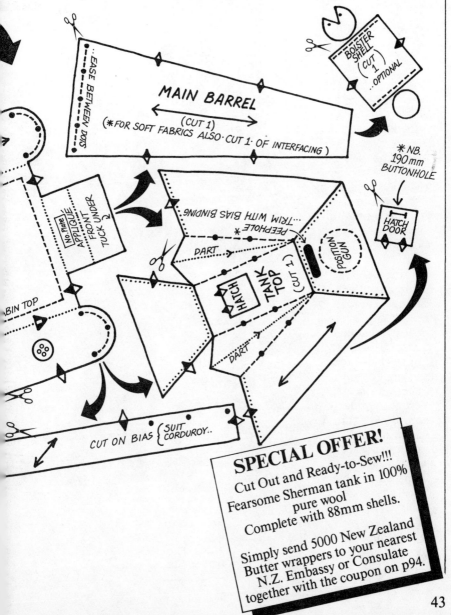

COMPOSE
NATIONAL

Be the envy of your neighbours and the talk of the local shopping centre . . . bring each day to a close with an anthem of your very own.

Imagine the scene . . . as the last television programme of the evening fades to a dot, your family and friends stand shoulder to shoulder in your front room and sing together, lustily, an anthem of your own creation to the piercing accompaniment of your quartz-powered singing calculator-cum-digital watch.

Feel your heart burst with pride as the strains of your very own anthem swell and die around the detritus of your dining room table after Christmas dinner.

Picture yourself standing on your balcony, waving to

44

YOUR OWN
ANTHEM

your lawn, wiping tears from your eyes as your pre-programmed, credit card-sized calculator plays your haunting refrain from deep within your jacket pocket.

Method:

1 Write lyrics, include references to your street, your house, your hobbies, your family and your pets. You might like to add a verse or two about your job, your mother-in-law and Uncle Charlie's little drink problem.

2 Using your singing calculator, compose tune. Try entering your bank balance divided by your birthday and multiplied by your postcode. Unless you have a very great deal of money in the bank, this should result in a lilting melody line that is particularly well-suited to a rousing iambic pentameter.

45

Here is an example of
a successful 'Personal
Anthem' penned by
Ron and Maureen
Dirge, who claim that
this song has changed
their lives:

*G*od save Ron and Maureen
God save Alf and Gayleen
God save our Gran
Da da da da
Care for our pussy cats
Goldfish and cricket bats
We've watered our cabbage patch
God help the beans.

Rousing stuff eh?

CORRIGAMI

The art of folding corrugated iron sheeting

In Japan, where everything is pretty small (apart from Sumo wrestlers and the fear of failure), people have contented themselves with dainty pastimes such as Hari-kiri (ritual suicide) and Origami (the art of folding little pieces of paper).

In Australia (no less artistic a nation despite rumours to the contrary) a sister craft has been flourishing since the days of Federation. This is a pastime for Bruce as well as Sheila and throughout the rugged outback one sees happy little Aussie lads and lasses gaily throwing corrugated iron darts and planes about the place, while their contented parents fill the long months between sheep-shearing contracts nimbly transforming rusted sheets of corrugated iron into fantastical, life-like sculptures of birds and flowers with which to decorate their homesteads.

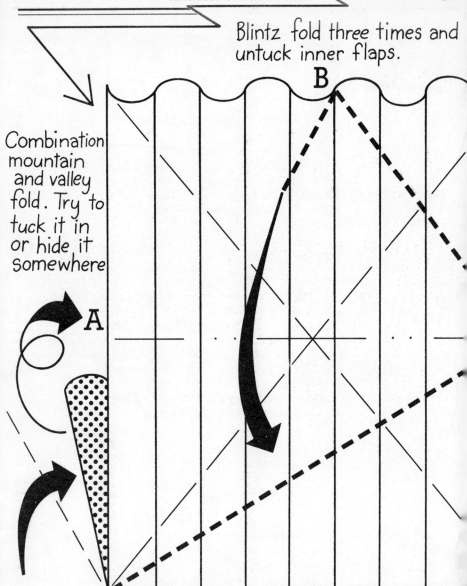

Blintz fold three times and untuck inner flaps.

B

Combination mountain and valley fold. Try to tuck it in or hide it somewhere

A

Lift up this base and reverse fold after e
alternate petal fold, sink any pieces left
and turn counterclockwise slightly. Pull
remaining corners and squash-fold back
If any of the crimp folds are showing st

If the stem section bends jump on it.

Crimp fold any little bits that stick out.

Corrigami, like Origami, entails only folding and tearing and eschews the use of scissors or paste. The following instructions will enable you to make a delicate lotus flower out of one 8ft (2.4384m) square sheet of slightly rusted corrugated iron.

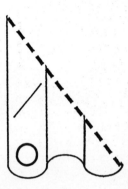

Tips:
Fold slowly and methodically, running along the fold line with the finger nails to ensure a crisp and accurate crease. When tearing corrugated iron, hold sheet in left hand if right-handed and in the right hand if left-handed. Grip gently but firmly between index finger and thumb, tearing in one swift continuous motion, taking great care not to go against the grain. Have a tetanus injection before you start.

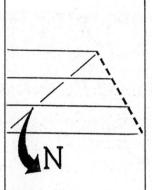

Method:
Fold the inside outside and the outside inside. Crimp fold the outside blintz fold and effect a double rabbit ear at each corner followed by a squashed petal fold across the centre line. Tear off excess to create a fine stem.
Shake out lotus flower.

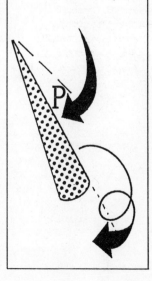

CORNER YOUR OWN

I n the high-flying world of commerce, the man (or woman) who corners the market is Queen (or King). Why? Because once you've bought up the world's supply of something then the world will beat a path to your door for that something and you can charge what you like. You simply cannot fail to get rich.

Human nature being what it is, people will always want what they can't have, even if it's something they don't want. Because a lot of experienced operators have cornered the more obvious commodities such as surgical trusses and knicker elastic, the beginner would be advised to start with something that there isn't a huge demand for.

Take chocolate-covered ants for example. While demand is not exactly overwhelming, it is steady.

How to Proceed:
1 Buy up all chocolate-covered ants from your local stores.

2 Order more.

(Repeat steps 1 and 2 until world supply is exhausted).

3 Publish revolutionary new diet book that proves instant fat loss is possible on an exclusive diet of chocolate-covered ants.

4 Sit back and wait for the money to roll in.

COMMODITY

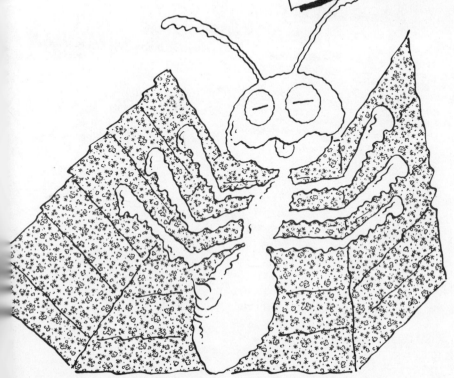

IMPORTANT ANNOUNCEMENT!

Two million copies of 'THE JOY OF ANTS — *The Instant Answer to Permanent Weight Loss*' are available at a huge discount from the publishers of this book. Your orders will be dealt with in the strictest confidence. ALSO . . . Take advantage of this NEVER-TO-BE-REPEATED offer . . . Cases of chocolate-covered ants at a knockdown price . . . BUY ONE, GET TWO FREE!! Delivery anywhere in the world. See p94 for details.

PERM YOUR OWN

It's time to put an end to those old Just-paid-the-orthodontist's-fees-and-it's-cost-me-one-month's-income-for-one-bloody-piece-of-chicken-wire Blues!

And you can do it and still have perfectly straight teeth!

HOW?

A revolutionary new discovery based on an age-old herbal remedy . . .

Deep in the Amazon jungle grows the wonder-herb everyone's talking about — *Allo there®*. It has many special medicinal properties which our chemists are working on around the clock.

The Amazon Indians have long known of its amazing tooth-softening properties. Once the teeth have been steeped in *Allo there®* for an hour or so, it is possible to straighten them up, or create an adorable 'buck tooth' look just for that special date . . . and joy of joys . . . you can 'do' your teeth as often as you like.

Our wonder-kit comprises:

1 bottle *Allo there®* tooth-perming lotion.
A set of clamps and pins.
A copy of 'The Complete Book of Tooth-perming'.
An instruction leaflet including 101 tooth-perming suggestions for special occasions.

Just send two months' wages along with the coupon on p94.

Your money back if not delighted!

TEETH

Genuine Testimonials:

"Since buying your . . . tooth-perming kit, I've had nothing but . . ."
C.P.

"I would like to . . . most vigorously about your . . . tooth-perming kit which has left me . . . My wife and children have . . . all thanks to your . . . product."
J.S.

"Your . . . product has . . . my life. You will be hearing from my lawyers."
R.R.

FIND YOUR OWN ATLANTIS

Few challenges are left to the adventurous spirit. Mount Everest has been climbed in the nude and the world has been circumnavigated in a leaky bathtub – it's difficult to get your name in the history books these days.

But here is a project that is bound to get you noticed...just imagine the headlines:

SMALL TOWN BOY FINDS BIG TIME CITY!

ATLANTIS AT LAST!

DARING DIVER DISCOVERS DEEP SEA "DALLAS"!

ILL-EQUIPPED IDIOT LOST AT SEA!

Equipment:
1 school atlas
1 compass
1 snorkel and mask
1 pr. flippers
1 or 2 books of South
American Legends
1 ball stout twine
1 boat (seaworthy)
1 companion
1 HB pencil
1 pkt. chewing gum

Method:

STEP TWO: Locate likely spot. Mark atlas boldly with an X.

STEP THREE: Set sail, remembering to take your companion, some honey and plenty of money and a bucket with a glass bottom.

STEP ONE: Read up on the lore and legends of South America. If any mention of Atlantis is made, underline. If using library book, insert a bookmark. Bits of Atlantis have been spotted (or not) by various people (so they say) and the general consensus of opinion is that it is located somewhere between South America and Africa, several thousand feet under the sea bed, with a few tall towers and such like sticking up through the silt.

STEP FOUR: Make sure you inform the nearest coastguard of your position and the editors of all Sunday newspapers of your intentions.

STEP FIVE: Gaze at sea bed through bottom of bucket until:
a) You cease to be newsworthy
b) You find a lost city
c) You strike oil

IRRIGATE YOUR OWN

I sn't it just the last straw? After all the hassle of getting the muesli and nut cutlets for supper, throwing the I Ching and putting the goat out, you're ready to settle down for the evening in the lotus position when you realise that you've forgotten to fill up all those little bowls of water that are dotted all around your lounge room in order to keep up the humidity level.

THIS NEED NEVER HAPPEN TO YOU AGAIN. NEVER.

All you have to do is install a permanent irrigation system in your home to keep up a level of humidity that a rain forest would be proud of. You will cut out for ever those irritating trips to the bathroom and the slop-slop-splish-splash involved in carrying all those little bowls about.

We are all aware of the ecological importance of living with rising damp. What with acres of rain forest being destroyed hourly, we must all do our bit to regenerate the earth's ozone layer. And another thing. Medical research has proved that the presence of water in the living area dampens the negative electrical neons (invisible rays from outer space) that cause the mind to rot, the body to weaken and thus lay itself open to all kinds of incurable syndromes.

LOUNGE ROOM

You will need:

Sufficient plastic tubing to engulf
your home
1 Archimedes screw
A nearby creek or river bed
An extremely gullible nature

Method:

Fix up screw and tubing using
beads and guitar strings to secure.

Turn to page 94 for advice on
getting rid of mildew, and look up
the recipe section for 101 delicious
ways with home-grown fungus.

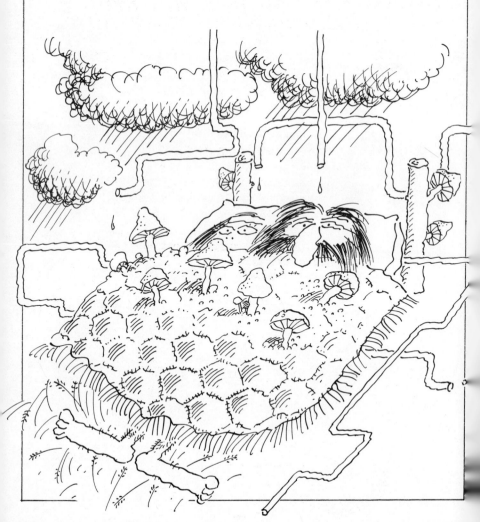

AMBUSH YOUR OWN HOME

Fall in for ambush tactics practice, quick smart ONE TWO, ONE TWO.

Whitewash family car, cat and anything else that moves.

Lop branches off nearby trees and affix to tin hats.

Camouflage self and other members of ambushing party in outfits unlikely to cause a stir in the neighbourhood. i.e. opal miners, stockbrokers, ballet dancers etc. Don tin hats.

Assemble ambush party in a clump of rose bushes. Point out (using Field Marshal's baton) exact whereabouts of home and rose bushes on map drawn up specially for this occasion.

Dig in, at all times keeping out of the line of fire. Position your bazookas, anti-aircraft guns and claymore mines in ambush position (see p. 102 of Karl von Clausewitz's well-known classic on the subject—an invaluable tome—no home is safe without one.)

Your home must suspect

nothing, act normally during these preparations.

In order to lure your home over to the rose bushes, make a detour in the front path, so that your home will, quite unsuspectingly, move towards your entrenched troops.

When you see the whites of the

62

net curtains...and not a moment before...let off coloured smoke grenades and, using the ensuing confusion to your advantage, attack fiercely yelling morale-boosting, plumbing-curdling slogans such as: "I'm coming for you...you yellow bellied bathtub!"

"I'll fix you, drain!"
"Take that, guttering!"

Send in the children to conduct mopping-up operations while you subdue the last pockets of resistance in the garage and other outbuildings.

Next time, remember your doorkey.

BRICK AF

Living and Dried Brick Arrangements to suit every occasion.

"Full many a brick is born to blush unseen And waste its sweetness on the desert air"
Lines from "Elegy Written in a Country Brickyard"

Most people start their brick-arranging experience as children picking wild bricks while out for a walk. These artless bunches of pavers and kerbstones are often put into whatever container is at hand – a hod

A right-angled, geometric abstract using horizontal quarry tiles and vertical mortar rakes. Note how the texture of the container is echoed in the footings by the asymetrical line of the damp-proof course.

propped up in the corner of the room or a jam jar on the kitchen window sill.

Gradually the realization dawns that the presence of bricks in the home elevates the spirit. Bricks console and bring happiness. Learning to arrange them helps to develop one's artistic gifts and induces feelings of tranquillity.

No special occasion would be complete without the additional adornment of a brick arrangement. Imagine a dinner party with no brick veneer piers...a wedding with no bouquet of tiles!!

Here are a few suggestions for brick arrangements to enhance typical occasions that occur in all our lives.

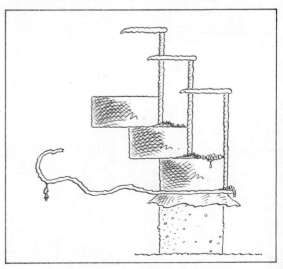

RANGING

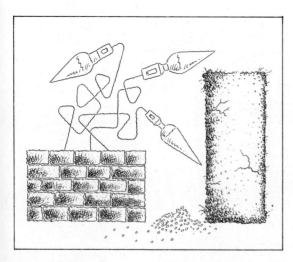

A dried arrangement – a rhythmic course of sandstock echoes the texture of the brooding, static mud bricks and an exuberance of pea gravel and plumb bobs highlight the meaningful juxaposition of flashings and footings.

The Formal Dinner
Bricks should complement the table setting and not clash with the decor or the food. The height of the arrangement will depend on the seating plan...after all, the last thing you want is for your guests to be hidden behind a pile of bricks. Two or three courses is usually sufficient. Remember that the arrangement will be seen from above, so concentrate on displaying your pointing and capping-off techniques. A touch of glycerine will add that extra sparkle.

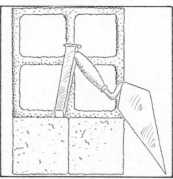

A thematic work entitled "Racial Tension in the Modern World". This is a beautifully staged piece – the warm colours of the pavers contrasting poignantly with the cold chisel and the pointing tool which are captured within the steely-grey confines of a cavity brick.

The Wedding

The wedding gives more scope to
the brick-arranger than perhaps
any other occasion. And as it's the
bride's day her choice of raw
materials should be considered. If
she should have a predilection for
handmades or commons, listen to
her and make these the theme of
your arrangement. Many brides
will find a pack of roofing tiles
makes a particularly romantic
bouquet. When assembling the
bouquets, do take into
consideration the height and
overall size of the bride—
a badly-balanced pile of
tiles could ruin the
whole effect.

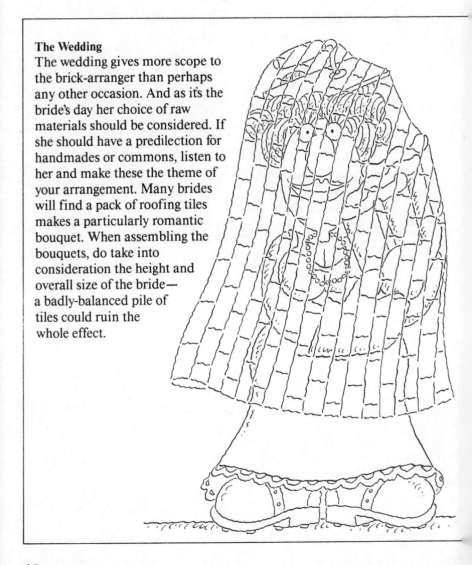

Meeting of the Sub-Aqua Club
How many times have you been to a meeting of the diving club only to be greeted by a blank space where a beautiful thematic pile of bricks could have been? Such a meeting presents real scope for the imaginative brick-arranger.
Imagine a fishing net draped artfully over a hod full of concrete blocks, a clutch of clinker bricks arranged to resemble a damp-proof course...but you will have ideas of your own!

In Conclusion
Plumb the air-cavities of your skill and imagination to find the right mix of lime and sand, of facings and footings. The art of brick-arrangement is, after all, an ephemeral thing, yet it undoubtedly adds to the sum of man's spiritual vision of the universe. A brick placed just "so" is enough to raise man's eyes heavenwards.

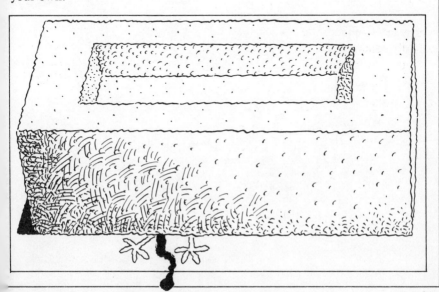

EMBALM
YOUR OWN CAR

A well-waxed, gleaming car is the ultimate status symbol. It says quite plainly to one's neighbours:

I am the sort of person who organises my time in such a way that I can spend every Sunday afternoon buffing the chrome and blacking the tyres. You slobs probably get drunk at lunchtime and waste the rest of the day sleeping it off.

Well have I got news for You!

Thanks to a revolutionary car-embalming fluid (a spin-off from the nuclear arms race) your car can enjoy a permanent gleam, and you can find some other excuse to avoid the washing up. You could go for a walk – you certainly won't be able to go for a drive because, as we all know, a car belongs in a nice, clean driveway, not on a filthy, dangerous, tar-spattered and dusty road.

Equipment:

1 Jumbo-sized can of embalming fluid`
1 pr. rubber gloves
Several large plastic garbage bags (black, preferably)
Hypodermic syringes in varying sizes
1 gift pack of car cosmetics
Body wax

Method:

1 Remove all messy bits from inside and underneath. Clean, inject with embalming fluid, pack neatly into garbage bags and return to body.

2 Spread a thin veil of wax evenly over body, buffing gently with a soft, black velvet cloth.

3. Make up body to look as it did in life.

4 Rest peacefully in the knowledge that your loved one will remain ever young and beautiful as you grow old and wrinkled. (c.f. **Dorian Ford** by the flamboyant Oscar Mercedes.)

VANDALISE YOUR OWN PHONE

It's make-over time again! Down with all those pretty-pretty flouncy curtains! Off with those wishy-washy marbleised wallpapers! To the garbage dump with last week's oh-so-tasteful throwover rugs!

This month's top decorator look is 'Neo-vandal-punk'. How can it be yours? Well rip up all your sheets, tear your carpet to ribbons, chip all your baths and basins and pour buckets of fluorescent yellow and pink paint over your three-piece suites. All the top people are 'punking it up' this month. Of course, it takes a trained eye to do it properly, and, as always, it is advisable to call in the experts. It is amazing how easily the whole scheme can go wrong and result in a hideous mess instead of an artful, *modèrne,* disorder with distinct intellectual overtones.

It is pointless to go half-way with a radical new look. You have to *live* fashion, and here are some 'Neo-vandal-punk' ideas that you can safely embark on yourself and save a whole lot of money on designer's fees.

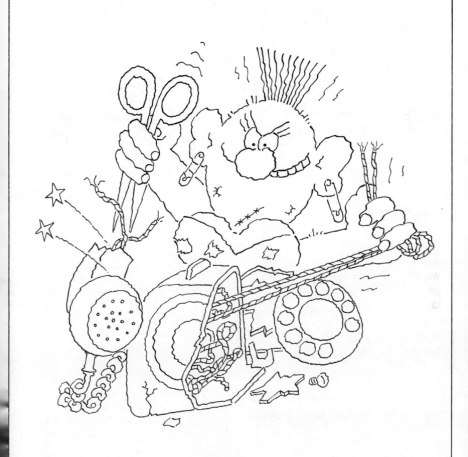

- Take an axe to your dishwasher and short-circuit your stove just before you give that IMPORTANT dinner party.
- Ram the toaster into the electric kettle, and snip off the plugs.
- Blend all your kitchen utensils in the Magimix.

- Wait until the appropriate moment (an imminent birth or heart attack) to vandalise your own phone by ripping the cord from the wall, snipping the curly wire with the kitchen scissors and prizing the dial out with a medium-sized, plastic-handled screwdriver.

Next month's look prediction: The Rural Landscape ... *includes 'How to house-train sheep', 'How to grow wheat furniture', 'Making silage in the urban bathroom' and mulch mulch more!*

PLOT YOUR OWN DOWNFALL

You'd be surprised how many people have succeeded at this beyond their wildest dreams:

Elvis Presley

Oscar Wilde

Snow-White's Step-mother

Try inviting this lot round
to dinner and see what
they come up with.

Cleopatra

Adam

The Duke
of Windsor

Rumpelstiltskin

Any Chinese politician
you care to name

Dumpty

Adolf Hitler

Eve

First, find Belgium.

COMPILE YOUR OWN BOOK OF WORLD FAMOUS BELGIANS

THIS LINE

BUCKWHEAT

AT
YOU
N'T
SEED
E
AGAIN

AGMENTS OF
EMISH CULTURE
UND HERE

Y ou cannot do this alone. Recruit one or two friends into a 'Name a famous Belgian' circle. Wait for the excitement to die down, get on with your lives and when the name of a famous Belgian slips into your mind, you must immediately ring up the other members of the circle NO MATTER WHAT THE HOUR.
Save the best until 4 a.m.

Rules:
1 Famous Flemish persons pre-1831 (the date of the founding of modern Belgium) are not considered Belgian for the purposes of this project.
2 Royalty don't count – we're after people who have achieved fame, not had it thrust upon them.
3 Looking up Belgians in reference books is not in the spirit of the thing, they must just occur to you.

This list will start you off. (Quite frankly, if you can add ONE memorable name to this lot, we will be extremely surprised...It is the result of three months intensive effort (without recourse to the library) by a circle of four frightfully talented, attractive and well-read people.

75

LIST

(In order of occurrence...)

TOOTS THIELMANS
Jazz harmonica player

JACKIE ICKX
Racing driver

EDDY MERCKX
Cyclist

THE SINGING NUN
(Say no more)

EDITH CAVELL
*Heroine of British origin but anyone who dies
for Belgium deserves a place on this list*

CESAR FRANCK
Composer

DJANGO REINHARDT
Jazz guitarist

BOBBY JASPER
Jazz flautist and saxophonist

FRANCY BOLLAND
Jazz band leader

OLIVIER GENDEBIEN
Racing driver

HENRI SPAAK
Politico

GASTON ROELANTS
Runner

EMILE PUTTEMANS
Runner

JULES BORDET
Nobel prize-winning immunologist

MAURICE MAETERLINCK
Playwright and poet

LUCIEN VAN IMP
Cyclist

HERCULE POIROT
*Fictional detective.
Actually, he was the first person we all thought
of, which proves conclusively that he has the
highest profile of any Belgian, living or dead. If
you were a Belgian, wouldn't you be concerned?*

N.B. Will this harm sales of the book in Belgium? Ed.

INDEX

A practical reference book such as this
without an index simply isn't on, is it? Here is
an extract from a really nice index, a bit of a
glossary and some particularly thought-
provoking instructions on the making of
pouffes.

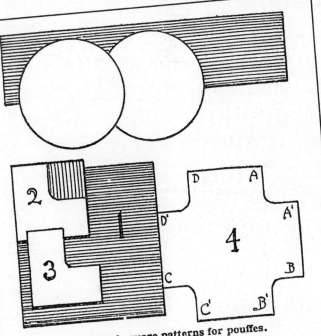

Round and square patterns for pouffes.

HOW TO MAKE A POUFFE

Pouffes give a room a very comfortable and cosy air; they are, moreover, very popular seats, as many people prefer them to chairs.

The diagrams show both the round and square pouffe; the round one is perhaps a little easier to make.

The materials required are as follows: unbleached calico, or ticking, for the case to hold the filling; white wool, or wool and fibre mixed, or stuffing from old mattresses, worn-out chairs, or old bolsters.

The method of making the case for the round pouffe is very similar to that used for a bolster. Having bought 1½ yards of calico, cut out two circles measuring 17 inches across, and a strip 66 × 13 inches.